"Out of the cacophonous multicultural clamor that we call America, Jim Hanson composes his provocative lyrics in a hero's effort to reach that which is ungraspable. He incorporates notes, chords, and themes, both harmonious and dissonant, from sources as varied as Plato and Lao Tzu, Einstein and Meister Eckhart, Saint John and Zoroaster, Heisenberg and Lucretius. Sometimes taking the role of Virgil, the guide, and other times, Dante, the seeker, Hanson accompanies us down the many strange byways of the human mind as it searches for the ineffable."

–William L. Holcomb, physician and founder of Heartland Zen Meditation Community of St Louis

"Jim Hanson's poems are about faith and the journey as a spiritual metaphor. While describing that in real life the way is often lost, he opens the way to salvation by the walking poems at the end. Great stuff."

–Hugh Muldoon, late poet and activist, Carbondale, Illinois

ENDLESS JOURNEY: POEMS IN SEARCH OF MEANING

Poems by Jim Hanson

Spartan Press

Spartan Press
Kansas City, Missouri

Spartan
Press

Copyright ©Jim Hanson, 2022

First Edition: 1 3 5 7 9 10 8 6 4 2

ISBN: 978-1-958182-04-8

LCCN: 2022939166

Cover image: *Wanderer above the Sea of Fog*, 1818, Caspar David
Friedrich; special thanks to the Kunsthalle art gallery.

Author photo: James Hanson

Acknowledgments

I owe much to the comments and encouragement of my friends and colleagues, the Duffers reading group, and especially Hugh Muldoon and Terry Russell, also to Carol for always being there, selflessly. Thank you.

Poems appearing elsewhere are found in:

"Tales of the Shrub," "Supersoul" as *Soul of Souls, Dissident Voice.*

"Cyber War Won," *Writers Resist.*

"Kermit's Demise," *Poetry Month,* Southern Chapter of Illinois State Poetry Society.

"Living Ghosts," *Nightingale and Sparrow,* No. 4.

"Meltdown," *Coastal Shelf: A Journal of Literary and Visual Arts,* Issue 3.

"Passing," *Harbinger Asylum* (journal of Transcendental Zero Press), Spring 2021.

"The River" / "The Survivors" as *Between Generations, I am not a silent poet.*

"Tipping Point," *Harbinger Asylum* (journal of Transcendental Zero Press).

Anthropic Musings: Poems on Human Survival in the Coming Extinction, Flutter Press.

"Let Him Ago" *Southern Chapter of the Illinois State Poetry Society.*

Table of Contents

I start out on this road,
call it love or emptiness.
I only know what's not here. . . .
I am somewhere lost in the wind.

– Rumi

I tramp a perpetual journey . . . .
Not I, not any one else can travel that road for you,
You must travel it yourself.
It is not far, and it is within reach.

– Walt Whitman

ENDLESS JOURNEY

LOST JOURNEY

We find no limit to our meager mind
beyond the stars where nothing will be ours
when the last line is crossed and journey lost.

. . . .

The journey calls you to adventure smelling of
lotus flowers at the feet of Gandhi marching to the salt flats
witnessing Paul's conversion on the road to Damascus
arising with Dante's soul from Inferno to Paradise

or to your own adventure to start another day
as you walk a path in the park and hear birds
calling forth thoughts to seek out unknown things

safeguarded by angels who travel with you
like Leonard Cohen wanting to travel with Suzanne
trusting your perfect body and mind along the way.

The journey takes you away from home to travel
over rocky paths, barren lands and hazardous places
through shadows of clouded days and shrouded darkness

often off course to the strange lands sailed by Odysseus
or places like Yeats' Byzantium not fit for old men.

Yet you know where to go and what turn to take
not by map route, compass direction, or GPS
by something within encoded in your DNA

and foretold in a dream of ominous image
shaking your body and shaping your mind

by something beyond drawing you forward
like a magnetic force felt in waves of energy
coming from forces of power not seen

and you want to walk through that golden gate
to view the world below as if you were God.

The journey turns and ends back home where
you are directed by the homing instinct
not heard but felt as an eternal return
in homage to the past brought back alive
from dreams that never die or answer why

old smells that perfume your consciousness
blurred mirrors that reflect ghostly faces
and haunting memories that linger in
this hallowed genesis of womb and home.

Your journey returns to life of time to relive.

. . . .

The dawn of day lights the way of the journey
with squinting brightness and awaking sounds

to eyes of the hero seeing truth and fame
over circumstance changed or windmills charged

or to ears hearing songs of birds calling
the spirit to go forth to destiny

or hearing the music of celestial spheres
in harmony with perfect fifth intervals

or smell of fragrances revived from
the past to recognize the future.

The journey marches to the beat of the heart
and each breath in and out in natural rhythm
twenty-four thousand for twenty-four hours
counting to begin again until the end

each breath a beat unnoticed but for
the old Zen master who sits silently

breathing in suffering of the world and
breathing out impurities of the mind

knowing each breath counts down samsara
between the start of day and end of night

knowing the journey is always endless
in time starting and ending as timeless.

. . . .

As the dusk of day fades to dark of night
when the journey ends at its storied rest

let us go then, you and I
when the evening spreads out against the ski

humming love songs with Prufrock through
half-deserted streets and muttered retreats

passing hand-in-hand dimly lit rooms where
women go speaking of Michelangelo

and we need not ask What is it?
simply go and make our visit

with Prufrock's poet growing old
when four quartets to God were told.

Yet we know our visit will descend
from the day to night and darker end

years wasted as life's measured meaning by
meters of rhythm and meaning of rhyme

stories depicting great journeys
still ending in dissolution

as white of day blinds and black of night finds
Homer blinded as Iliad hero

Milton blinded in paradise lost and
Oedipus self-blinded seeking vengeance

as illusions of heroic journeys
become disillusions of prosody.

. . . .

The journey of spheres and stars was
once the steady state of heaven
claimed by religious orthodoxy
and mathematical constancy.

This the church fathers knew was surely true
as the center for all God oversaw and
although Copernicus decentered the earth
Newton restored order by natural laws.
– a happy emotion

until Hubble broke the bubble
of a steady state universe
and observed it running rampant
from the cosmological constant

his unwelcome observation
of speeding toward oblivion
through time made asymmetrical
and space beyond mass made straight by

chaotic forces undetected
with dark energy suspected
making equations very odd
for the perfect universe of God

– a hapless commotion.

What the church fathers knew no longer is true
as faith evaporates and prayer dissipates
portending the godless second coming
of Yeats' beast slouching toward Bethlehem

in a world not there to make or take
rather a mystery that begins and ends
coming as particles from the Big Bang and
going as galaxies out to the Big Freeze
– a faithless motion.

. . . .

Spirit starts with doubt of faith
to reform and upgrade history:
Moses through the Red Sea to the Promised Land
– chosen people to save
Jesus from the Mount of Olives to Jerusalem
– resurrection from the grave
Muhammad with the hijra from Mecca to Medina
– holy empire to crave.

Spirit ends with faith of doubt
to deform and degrade history:
Napoleon on the low road to Paris
 – republic to make and break
Lenin on the high road to Moscow
– republic to fake

America on the way to world empire
– republic to forsake (like Rome).

Spirit dies in institutions when:
politics beholds the end of history and ideology
industrial plutocracy underwrites civic democracy
media platforms create a digital paradise
global commerce flattens a diverse world
civilizations clash through bank funds and cyber wars
postmodern imperialism rides high trade winds.

Spirit dies in people when:
billionaires praised as philanthropists
pilgrims migrate to save heathen souls
historians forget Gibbons' fall of empire
believers deny being Nietzsche's Last Man
national leaders fail to heed Orwell's 1984
corporate captains deny the Anthropocene Age.

You want it darker
We kill the flame.
           – Leonard Cohen

. . . .

Science journeys into endless frontiers
remembering Vannever Bush's clarion call
to chalk upon blackboards squeaky and square
universal theories of everything

from the infinite of astrophysics to
infinitesimal of quantum physics

from Plato's eternal certainties to
Heisenberg's particles of chance

from Darwin's competition of the fittest
to E.O. Wilson's cooperation of the ants

from Skinner's conditioned behavior
to Maslow's self actualization.

The scientific method travels all roads to
correct thoughts of common experience
debunk hoary myths of traditional insight
demystify beliefs not counted and mounted

yet forgetting Lao Tzu's call to lose knowledge
of measured judgments thought to be certain and
to attain the quiet harmony of Tao
that gives and takes all things in heaven and earth.

. . . .

Looking far, he was with a star
Looking down, he was on the ground
I saw that pale adventurer of a thousand faces
The intrepid traveler from ten thousand places.

I asked,
from where he comes
to where he goes.
He replied,
from star stuff he comes
to carbon dust he goes.

I asked,
if he were a god or avatar.
He replied,
a soul over human sense
of cosmic providence.

I asked,
about Eden
and about Heaven.
He replied,
'twas a mishap
never on the map.

I asked,
about the purpose of life
and finality of death.
He replied,
both are a mystery
solved only by me.
I asked,
if I could learn
about his sojourn.

He replied,
no need to ask
'tis already your task.

Yes, I am the unnamed traveler of all places
The unheralded hero of a thousand faces
Reliving a life of changing form
Whereby the old go as youth reborn.

. . . .

To find my way I could not stay.
The house became yet smaller and
the walls spoke of time passed away
from youthful hopes of leaving old
photo-paintings by Norman Rockwell.

Traveled east up the state highway
to cities unknown, opportunities untested

for a college degree, resume
money-making career, deferred funds
with rented rooms, impersonal jobs,
passing voices slurred, faces blurred.

When talking to nameless people
I began to whisper to myself:

take leave of this noisy place
about no one but everyone
belonging out somewhere else,
and go back where you belong.

Traveled west from cities unknown
leaving behind people still unnamed.

I come to stay and find my way.
The house becomes ever larger
and the streets speak of time passing
with real people having last names
and faces in high school yearbooks.

. . . .

When the last line is crossed and journey lost
we find no limit to our meager mind
beyond the stars where nothing will be ours.

SEARCH FOR MEANING

WAYS OF THE PATH

I am somewhere lost in the wind.

– Rumi

Walk down the park pathway and
smell flowers in nectar breeze
hear the call from trees around
see opening light ahead
march upon hallowed ground

like pilgrims everywhere
Muslims to Mecca and paradise of Allah
Christians to Jerusalem and heaven of God
Buddhists on Veda Day off to nirvana.

Venture up into the vista and
ride the whirlwind with Rumi
do the dervish dance with Shams
lose yourself in formless sand
release spirit in open sky

where few souls would want to fly
letting go of the world below
getting lost in free emptiness
going far and free of gravity.

Venture not back to your home where
they know not who you are or what you mean
although you want to be of good health to them
as you recite the Whitman song of self

here in Kansas where the wind is
but weather and possible rain
for flat fields of wheat.

Ride not on the road with poetic Beats
sullied children of New York city streets
seeking refuge from authority
being led into hell by Bill Burroughs

this William Tell Burroughs
drugged in Mexico City
shooting his wife in the head.

Listen not with Vivekananda to
Madam Calve sitting on her veranda
and lamenting her fear of becoming a
drop of water lost in the Indian Ocean

sitting with Rudyard Kipling
and sipping Lipton Tea
British to the last.

Stride not down from the mountain
with Zarathustra to foretell the world
of the great liberating noontide

yet spurned and turned away
condemned to end his life
in the madness of night.

Stay not with old Robinson Jeffers
warning those who would partake in
Mother Church and Father State when
nothing good can be understood

> it being too lonely to be an adult
> to California children who
> march on pictured sunny shores
> Rainbow Sandals on their heads
> bodies tanned with Natural Glow
> arms tattooed with Taijitu
> chanting Tao as good monks do.

Plead not in song with Leonard Cohen
singing on high from his tower of song
commiserating with Hank Williams
how love was lost and what went wrong

> still singing high from his tower
> clinging to poetic power
> as his song goes through the night
> looking for love beyond his sight.

Listen not to beguiling mediums
of reason and data and lined by
postmodern computer directories
and maligned by webs of algorithms

> where instant truths are anecdotes
> what becomes viral is virtue

and the right face matters
how to look in the book.

The chosen path up the mountain
is narrow, weeded over and rocks under foot
yet followed by gods and heroes of old
of journeys taken in stories long ago told.

Ascend to the Egyptian wind gods
of all four directions, with Amun
the creator who ruled as the great
Protector of the Road to purity

men then blown away as formless sand
by the endless wind of history
erasing paths for human egos
and lifting poets of all ages

to now lost worlds traveled long ago.

BORGES' LIBRARY

Of making many books there is no end
– Ecclesiastes, 12-12

Borges and I are colleagues
who read books together

> in the library of Babel
> holding all books ever written.

We have a covenant much like
Doctor Faust and the Devil

> my soul given now
> to be returned when

> I find and read the
> last and highest book.

I ascend rooms and levels much like
Dante in the Divine Comedy

> surveying all that is
> written through the ages

> cave dwellers etching walls
> scribes chiseling tablets
> gods dictating to prophets
> imperialists reading Rosetta Stone

professors dictating textbooks
muses seducing paperback writers
moguls hawking yellow news
nerds programming digital texts.

I trudge up still higher taking
one stair and level at a time

books left below
knowledge attained

free of impending death
soul ascending saved

straight up to find love
for what may be seen
Jesus standing above
or maybe Joel Osteen.

I climb to the top and into the last room
empty of all books until I look up to

see the highest one
burning in the sun

as eternal flame
without soul or name

as ashes fall down
to remake the ground.

ANTHROPIC PRINCIPLE

No matter weak or strong, short or long
behold the Anthropic Principle
that is of you because you are of it

guided through an umbilical chord
born as star stuff from super novae
formed into a perfect small blue dot

thereby evolving through four eons
of four billion years then Cambrian life
from sea to land and matter to mind

language reflecting real forms
technology using four forces
science disclosing laws of nature

truth securing order and constancy
beauty assuring love and perfection
goodness inuring justice and morality

rising to transcendent consciousness
of primal causes and final effects
of all nature's laws for you and it.

MISANTHROPIC PRINCIPLE

Not about us as a grain of sand:

Cosmic egg that fried
universe that arose
constant laws that applied
cosmic rock that froze
energy that lived and died,

planets and asteroids colliding
stars birthing and dying in cataclysmic silence
supernovae spreading across light years
galaxies shattering the cosmological constant
and speeding into infinity,

billions of stars more numerous
than grains of sand on earth
trillions of planets – 99.9∞ percent arid
matter 99. 9∞ percent entropic
energy 99. 9∞ percent nihilative,

atoms entangled and elements ejected
photons emitted from
fusion of hydrogen to helium
gravitons emitted from
fission of atoms to particles,

A: A = A, A: A ≠ B
2+2 = 4

$A2 + B2 = C2$
$B = QA + R$
$E = MC2,$

already there
only universal law
earth water fire air
no purpose or care
no human error or flaw.

All about it as a desert of sand.

ANTHROPIC CHOCOLATE

We know matter is constructed
through the world of mind.

We know mind constructs
through the universe of matter.

We say about matter, never mind.
We say about mind, no matter.

Brain puts together matter and mind
mixing them as qualia of one kind.

Brain knows them as M&Ms
with human nuts added – cracked.

A WORD

A word of the journey was heard:

about Achilles and Odysseus
seeking fame and dominion

by proud poets going back to Homer
touting heroes of a thousand faces

in telling each journey as a story
of happy news and great man history

with inspiring ideology
and enduring immortality.

But the first word was blurred:

in the epic of history's first hero
Gilgamesh who journeyed for fame in vain

who doomed Endiku to early mortality
and failed to obtain his own immortality

who returned to Uruk to seek forgiving
and whiled away his last time of living

peeling an onion and crying no less
to find in the center mere nothingness.

And the last word of journey now is slurred
of heroes lauded for their wealth and rule

in their quest of dominance and progress
over the earth and nature turned cruel.

THE WORD

In the beginning was The Word

      said by God from on high to
      fill the void and light darkness

      then heard by Adam in Eden
      to learn about good and evil.

      What if

      God cut down
      to YHWH annulling the Rebus Principle

      Word cut first
      from guttural burbs and grunts expressed by ape
      not god

      Word cut up
      by Bill Burroughs from scriptures to letters and
      spun as Newspeak

      World cut back
      from Anthropocene Age back to Cambrian
      Period.

      What if

      the word was never heard
      instead nothing was said

the word never in conversation
only impulsive motivation

the word and world never the same
order and meaning never came.

What if all the above were that smart, at least in part?

OUT THERE

They are out there
in the black of space trillions of miles away
there on millions of planets
following a Cinderella path and rounding stars
tiny marbles with blue water and green life

there consisting of the elements of star stuff
oxygen, hydrogen, nitrogen and phosphorus
evolved as bacteria and multiple cells
central nervous systems
brains with sensory organs
minds with images abstracted
through the Rebus Principle
to create symbols of intelligence

– just like us
but perhaps evolved with brains and minds
a million years before us to know
things only our visionaries dream:

the theory of everything
completeness of logic and mathematics
certainty of positive language
self-actualization of individuals
united justice of societies
unity of duality

– not like us
perhaps to know things
in our future to come
not even our visionaries can dream:

primal start and final end of the universe
another universe of unknown dimensions
eternity of time, infinity of space
death before life, life after death
the smile of God.

Like them out there
we are here
with infinite possibilities.

TIME

BETWEEN GENERATIONS

Boomers die in tall buildings with small windows
fewer coming out than going in, coming out
with canes on good days, walkers on bad days
shuffling through doors of restaurants and stores
slowing down millennials in the bustle of bodies.

Millennials now earn their generational turn
swiping iPads and clicking icons of wonder
entering books of faces and looks of virtual places
media makings of texted logs and on-line blogs
and pop music with 1-5-4-1 chords to cheering hoards

> making the world flat
> Virtual for real
> Internet for free
> Digits for widgets
> GPS for God.

Their digits and dreams of futures soar through space
riding a vapor trail across the electromagnetic sky
circling 'round the globe on a silicon disc
reducing the world to a Microsoft chip
transmitting genes through the motherboard

> loving the world back
> Twitter me
> Facebook friends
> Circuits integrated
> Internet connectivity.

Forget Yeats and old men who never sailed to the new
   Byzantium
who reminisce about old wars, white movie stars and athletes
good days of dancing in music halls, drinking beer for a
   quarter
working for four dollars an hour and two-week vacations a
   year,
old men who cough and die within the walls of small houses
nursed by old women left alone in houses called home
gone in their time, always the same.

Yet Byzantium succumbed to its unpurged images
as will the postmodern day of unpurged icons
when data clouds disappear out beyond the Internet
and websites are condemned to the Wayback Machine,
each generation folding back into history as melted snowflakes
coming and going through the Grand Hotel of dreams
true in our time, always the same.

All things begin to end and end to begin as
earth turns to brown and sky turns black
each in its time to regain green and blue
the hues of time passing back to return as
the tape rewinds to show evolving generations
nothing changes but history turned old and recycled
true in all time, always the same.

ALREADY SAID

What did you say?

I cannot say it again.

I already spoke
  back there then.
My words once spoke
  are lost forever.

There is no now
  as if time stops.
There is only then
  as time goes.

What I say and do
  has already happened
as a past moving
  through the time of space.

The same words are
  not the same again
not the same again
  the same always different.

Do you hear me now?

No, you already spoke.

ONE TIME

Two roads diverged in a yellow wood,
And sorry I could not travel both

– Robert Frost, Road Not Taken

There is only one choice made for
youthful passions running all directions:

> in departure from home to places unknown
> in love with somebody there at the time
> in college curricula stamping career degrees
> in jobs with wary strangers and scary bosses.

There is only one choice, left by
fleeting seasons and lost chances:

> no do-overs re-dos replays retracts come-backs
> no life or parallel lives as in heroic novels
> no time-outs to weight and measure opportunities
> no holding what was in the present already gone.

What if freed for another love or deed
could should would have been said and done of
possibilities still unsaid undone?

No, there was but one preemptive choice
only one pivotal turn already tried and
taken by hard habit and soft convenience.
Many loves and deeds were thought to be
but the one life lived passed as history:

opportunities frittered and splintered away
dalliances of yet another passing day
so little so much, too early too late
one choice for one life at a one time.

The old man finishes his poem.
Drinks the bourbon in his glass.
Rises to walk across the room.
Lies in bed of egressing sleep.
Recalls his mother's fading words:
I think only of your happiness.

TIME TALK

You ask

if I have the time.

I say, Yes

I have it.

I then say, No

I don't have it.

I had it

but just lost it.

It was here

but now it's gone.

You ask again

if I have the time.

I say again

I'm always losing it.

If you want the time

get it yourself.

And if you do

give some to me.

Give what I just lost

talking to you.

I'm out of time

and you owe me.

So come back tomorrow

when you have time.

NEVER THERE

You hear the freight train
          sound coming low
          then going high

waves of sound
          rippling through the air

               between
                    the relativity
                    of time and motion.

You are only here
          by yourself
          to hear as

                    a lone station
                    in time and space.

You are never there
                    with the train

          which already left
          on tracks now silent.

SUFFERING OF LIVING

THE SURVIVORS

Look up. The Ik stand on high mountains formed long ago
as ghosts in shukas fluttering in timeless wind
silent reminders of tormented survival:

> motionless bodies of mountain stone
> gaunt faces of frozen granite
> eyes emptied of desire and hope
> under a purple sky and falling sun.

In the valley below the RVs trek their way on
dusty trails back to city hotels and restaurants
tourists taking full view of the African zoo:

> animals and vistas seen through IPhones
> live adventures through Twitter and Skype
> the thrill of hatari for tourist spenders
> assuring IMF payments for global finance.

The Ik stand as once proud warriors and hunters who
roamed freely across plush savannas as lions and
kings feasting on their domain and feared by rivals

> now driven away like hyenas at a lion kill
> from fertile valleys and nourishing waters
> unto the purgatory of barren mountains.

They slink down to hunt in darkness under police guns
hunted hunters risking life for meat and survival
competing with park animals kept for tourist cash

down from hard crags not fit for human feet
eating gaunt goats and acacia shrubs
existing in a land of stones and stick huts.

They loose hold of common humanity
treading upon death when dead already
civilization far out of their reach:

declining to live as Rousseau's noble savage
descending to instincts of ignoble savagery
deserting compassion and passion for living.

Befallen like the Ik, we also will reek:
pollution of global lands laid flat by corporate hands
cities glutted by populations and flooded by warming oceans
wars for dying and consumer whores for buying
demagogues fooling people and ruling markets.

Damocles' sword sways over our head
held just above by a slender thread
to fall and slice our humanity away
in just one day of world financial panic
global markets bleeding trillions of currencies
to rejoin nature as Darwin's descent of man.

Look again. The Ik still stand on high mountains
reminders of no life beginning and death ending
only stillness and silence, no sound of defiance.

THE FORAGERS

Maasai men walk on fields
of the Tanzanian plains
once fertile with grass and game
nourishing great mammals

now parched and cracked
by advancing desert
streaming down like the sun
of the equatorial north.

They stalk across the fields
their eyes fixed to the ground
searching morsels grown or thrown
below white-back vultures above

so many hungry down below
yet appearing middle class
wearing message t-shirts
and endorsed tennis shoes

and holding to their cheeks
to hear and speak aloud through
cell phones glistening in the sun
transmitting up to satellites

these world citizens speaking Bantu
across the digitized flat world
leveled by the unknown chieftains
of faraway billionaire tribes.

THE CARRIERS

You can look along the road to Arusha
beneath Mount Kilimanjaro to see
Maasai women walking early morning miles

as a Saturday parade marching
in their boubous flowing in the wind
showing colors of red and purple

young figures tall erect and proud
moving with the grace of models
on show at the Paris fashion week

(the models of haute couture
beautifying world womanhood
carrying champagne glass in hand).

You see them defying the sun
bodies shimmering through heat waves
arising from the outstretched land

carry by hand and on head
clay vessels filled with water
once pure from the mountain streams

stagnated since the last rain
now colored brown in small pools
for drinking by native beasts

but not for your drinking as the
onlooker imbibing in the
illusions of African beauty.

THE POOR

no one there

abandoned road
aching cold
dim light

shadows of fright

spoiling trash
whiskey mash
urine slime
alley grime

creatures homeless nameless
figures scuttled huddled
foul fires of garbage pyres
hazy stare of dirty air

empty figures
exhausted rigors
tossed
lost
no face
no place
jesus saves
only in graves

no heaven on earth
no place of mirth
no music of faraway sounds
no glow of barren grounds
no smell of flowers blooming
no feel of hands grooming
no hope or future
no warmth or nurture

no one there to care

TIPPING POINT

You walk away
upon dead grass turned brown
and down an empty field
under an overcast day awaiting winter
becoming smaller as you walk
alone into a gray clouded horizon.

Cold wind blows against my face
as I watch
standing stricken
feeling your pain
eating at my insides
hurting from the force of your hatred.

I want to be left alone by you
truly I do
to be done with the wrenching pain
you inflict upon me
and my panic from your screaming fury
beyond reason or words.

Yet knowing your despair
I want to follow and recant
make a last plea
right my wrong
sooth your hurt
and blunt your rage
if you would stop just this moment
to see and hear me and forgive.

But you walk on without looking back
limping and wounded
as I shout out into the night and cold
but too late
you disappear into the darkness.

I go back to the house
pour bourbon and sit
on a wooden chair in the dark
before an open window
as the sleet blows in hard and cold
wondering where you are
and if you are warm and well.

The horn of a train
sounds in the distance high and shrill
then goes low in passing
and fades away into the night,
and I shut the window
closing in silence
the tipping point passed.

WHAT HAPPENED?

I'm alone
                abandoned
my world fallen
                to the ground
its walls leveled
                nothing left
no Phoenix

                to rise over
ashes of fiery rage

                smoldering ruins
without an ember of hope.

I look at
                the ruins
now lifeless
                exposed to
what happened
                that night
when it all blew up

                before dim
reason falling to passion

                far stars of
love poisoned by hate.

I tried to stop and rewind the film
to redo the scene of a surreal rehearsal
– Hear me out! –
to undo the celluloid fire out of control
with a tragic end of what became real.

I tried to recant and redo the deed
to save something from the destruction
– I love you! –
from the rage burning bridges of hope
and to undo what had been done.

One life
       to live
one love
       to give
who is
       now lost
back then
       with you
that night.

The question won't stop.

What happened that night?

LIVING GHOSTS

Ghosts engender all of us
and live in our civilization
– so read a book, watch a movie, recall a line or speech or
historical event, look at a great skyscraper or jet airliner.

All came from those of the past – studying and
experimenting, developing their talent, breaking down old
forms and creating new ones, dreaming of the ideal form,
celebrating their genius, sparkling with youthful energy,
disdaining any limit on themselves, and assuming as do
we their life and age to be quintessential. They composed,
performed, wrote, painted, composed, acted, designed,
engineered, deliberated, legislated – creating civilization,
our civilization.

(And we come as their careless caretakers, redacting and
revising their works, defiling the primary with the
secondary, reinterpreting their dictums of truth, beauty
and goodness with the hermeneutics of postmodernism,
misinterpreting the flame of eternity for the flux of
modernity, acting as corrosive as the acids of nature,
listening to Glenn Gould play Bach and Al Pacino perform
Shakespeare – defiling authenticity, our replicability.)

Ghosts also engender each of us
and live in our home
– stay up late, turn out the lights, drink a whiskey, watch an
old movie, see actors long dead appear in the dark.

I watch a late-night movie with Fred Astaire dancing
sweetly with Ginger Rogers, gliding across the black/white
screen, brightening the drudgery of the thirties. And

not alone – yes, my father and mother are here, from a
long time past, in this moment of suspended disbelief.
We sit on the couch and talk about the good times
when dancing the jitterbug, singing the tunes of
Broadway, listening to Jack Benny; also surviving the
hard times of bankruptcies and strikes during the
depression, the dust storms of the great Plains, and
rations during the war. My mother recalls working
nights at a roadside café for 25¢ an hour, which was the
price of a movie ticket, and there she met my father a
truck driver. My father talks, too, about Model T cars
and Clydesdale trucks, about FDR and Eisenhower. I
offer cocktails, but the movie ends, and they rise from
the couch. No, please stay; we have so much to talk
about. But no use; the more I plead and attempt to hold
them, the farther they drift away, phantoms fading in
the late night air. Past and present tear apart, silently,
leaving no trace of what once was.

Ghosts live at night after day is done
when then and now occur as one.
At dawn of day they go away
to where I know I too will go.

PASSING

Seen through a looking glass
in light of every day

people pass in silence
in an unbroken file

going forward always
dull eyes staring ahead

seeking home for rest and
solace within still walls

or looking for love of
a short day or long life

or reaching the rainbow
for gold had at the end,

but reasons matter not
only passing matters

on trails trodden by beast
and prehistoric man

on roads of dirt trails
by oxen and horses

on highways of hard oil
as machines belch and roll

passing through all eras
of the anthropocene

across land unmoved through
hills formed epochs ago

into the wind blowing
over roads of no end

as gray sky turns to black
and light recedes to dark

seen the same as before
out through the looking glass

when passing comes to end
and to begin again.

ARE WE SAFE?

Celebrating our Prufrock love song
you and I go under a falling night sky
through certain half-deserted streets
by muttering retreats and old ladies
who come and go speaking of Michelangelo,

but we end in a dark place where the
grime of the street grinds beneath our feet
and the smell of damp ash and rotting flesh
hang bare in suffocating air.

We look to find a way out of
this portending place closed by labyrinthine walls
with windows of no light and doors of no escape
where nothing is heard but the cry of sirens passing by,

and breathing in and out to gasp for air
and from the dark reaching to grasp my hand
you ask in a voice far away in space:
Are we safe?

COLORS OF AGE

Years of age
are not gold
not silver
not even white.

They are
green turned to brown
white turned to gray
all ending in black.

SEASONS

Spring blooms and buzzes in warm confusion
breeding wild strawberries and future dreams
mixing budding growth and stirring schemes.

Summer arouses passions of thriving
hot projects of yearning for family
credentialing schools for prosperity.

Fall secures portfolio earnings and savings
deferment and insurance for posterity
career and middle-age practicality.

Winter is the cruelest season, chilling dreams when
freezing away what could would should have been
cold demise bringing on old departing sighs.

So the seasons will have come and gone
each a promise of something new yet
a recycle of what to regret

unfolding like an accordion playing
a wistful ode for folks of an old country
long buried roots under the family tree

bringing birth in spring and death in winter
shaping and coloring life in between
until beginning is ending serene.

VIOLENCE OF LIVING

TRIBE

The beast in the amygdala lies coiled
silent but watchful and easily aroused
by the movement of nature's ancient rivals.

It strikes out against threats to genetic purity
as males kill males for breeding intra-species
as males unite for killing inter-species.

Darwinians expound on primate killing to survive
but not on homo sapien killing for supremacy over
Neanderthals in Eurasia an epoch ago.

Modern Darwinians expound on ordered food chains
kept in ecological balance by Keystone Species
until at the top arrived the human Tombstone Species.

There was no mystery why the Neanderthals perished:
We the homo sapiens killed them, every one of them
down to the last mother and baby not of our species.

There is no mystery about persistent ethnic cleansing:
We kill those not of our clan and culture – with rival identities,
strange nurturing, alien languages, and odd gods – all of them.

Those who expound on human progress fail to ask:
Without the instinct to kill those not of us, would we be
Homo-neanders still learning about fire, wheel, and seed?

EVIL DONE

Kill the evil-doers
before they kill us.
Good does as evil done
justice done for everyone.

    Justice done by Chris Kyle
    for 9-11 terrorist payback through
    the cross hairs of a .300 Win Mag.

Evil begins with the story of Eden
with Adam the flawed dupe of creation
and Eve the innocent so tempting as
God tests the challenge of good with evil.

    255 kills done by Chris Kyles in
    the Arabic desert as an American
    sniper record to end world terrorist fear.

Sophocles tells the story through Ajax
killing Trojans, sheep as comrades, then himself
Greek hero of mad confusion struck down by
the classic infusion of good by evil.

    Good done by evil to Chris Kyle
    American hero gone home
    out on a Texas shooting range.

Evil marches on blood-soaked sand of Arabia:
Christian soldiers stay and snipe with bullet and drone
Muslim solders pray and bomb in fervent bliss
both promised virgins in a tanker of oil.

    Shot six times done by a brother Marine
    his PTSD gone mad still at war to
    kill his own deluded terrorism.

The voices still can be heard coming from
the ever wind-swept dunes of the desert
repeating the story of nothing learned
by those condemned to relive history.

CYBER WAR WON

Attention Americans!
War is now Peace.
Connectivity is Security.

The First World Cyber War
to have the final virus
and end all wars is won.

As you read this news:

You are selected for cyber security
as a digitized node on the Internet
and consumer of infinite data clouds.

You are protected from spyware and malware
by having passwords to authorized websites
and to assure access and guarantee privacy.

You are excepted from the foreign viruses
as bears and dragons are deleted and dumped
in recycled bins with the click of a key.

You are elected as the privileged user
of the world-wide cyber feedback system
made secure by Prism program surveillance.

You are connected – no need to get off line.
Everything is on line, every user included.
Nothing exists outside the digital text.

You are

       channeled to

       www.wifi.com

           figured in

           0's and 1's

               reduced to

               bits and bites

                   exiled to

                   infinite clouds.

Sleep well with Orwell.

You are being

Looked after.

LAST RIDE

Down from the mountains in the west the
wind blows through the rodeo corral

as old men sit on wooden fences
chewing Skoal talking of the old days

when the mountains were higher and
the days better when there never was

a bronco that could not be rode
a cowboy who could not be throw'd.

Casey climbs the steel bars of the chute and
sits on the vibrating back of the beast

takes a deep breath and gives his last nod and
the gate swings open and beast crashes out

violence erupts from beneath as he digs
his spurs into flesh and rope-hand holds fast

his body whip-lashing forward and back
from the beast-muscled thrust of g-forces

images flashing through blurred spaces as
he leaves behind the whirling arena

riding high on Zeno's arrow of time
for eight seconds lasting a life in his time

then falling down beneath gnashing hoofs
bringing to end the time of his life.

Of that time of old and the story is told
now by the men who still remember when

a ghost rider in the sky riding through
that last astral gate to enshrine his fate.

SWEPT AWAY

A spider
crawls up dark walls
spins its sticky web
kills its tangled prey
secures its silky world
hanging by a thread
of its own making

until swept away
by a broom made by

A human
builds up high walls
defends his land
kills his trespassers
secures his boundaries
hanging by a treaty
of his own making

until swept away
by another man.

So go schemes
of spiders and men
weaving clashing worlds
of their own making

walls of men

wars of nations

swept away.

gang aft agley.

EMPIRE

Herodotus sits on Mount Olympus
the gods now dead and legends gone
yet his works survive still this world
the father of history said so by Cicero.

From his view on high the centuries roll by
in time-lapse history always the same as
the sun above shines light and energy and
below storms of human conquest cross the planet
drenching green land with red blood and
lighting horizons with golden glory.

The great empires rise and fall over the
millennial ashes of fiery history
from Egyptian pharaohs to Microsoft wizards
their moment lauded universal and supreme
to end history – *temporis aeterni*.

They rise in bright ages of word and wisdom
from philosopher kings of the axial age
walking down rivers of civilization
as harbingers of art and industry
and moralists of justice and love

their fall in dark ages of violence
by the conquerors of order and power
speaking war is peace, ignorance is strength

as imperial capitals rise and fall
– Troy, Nineveh, Athens, Carthage,
Rome, Constantinople, Tenochtitlán,
Beijing, Berlin, Tokyo

their rise and fall always the same
extorting taxes, exhorting order, exalting gods,
wielding weapons of stone, bronze and iron,
machines, uranium and silicone.

Now comes the greatest since Rome as the
exceptional shining republic of citizens
bestowed with liberty and justice for all
as states united – *e pluribus unum*

inspired by Caesars of Pax Romana
now by presidents of industrial democracy
proclaiming free world leadership
as west to east as north over south
around the world to have and do

fulfilling Plato's prophecy of government
from aristocracy to democracy to tyranny.
fulfilling Gibbon's cycle of civilization
from birth to growth to death.

During the first rising of empire, when asked
why Greeks and Barbarians war against each other
Herodotus would say only, as a true Greek:
It ever was to be, always empire to seek.

LOST EARTH

MELTDOWN

We first met standing out
in the New York cold
unable to buy tickets
to see Neil deGrasse Tyson.
We walked through the snow
and you slipped on the ice
and I caught and held you
for a precious moment.
We found a warm coffee house
and talked about astrophysics
and you quipped about Mars as
a living option to a polluted
overheated earth perhaps even
the moon with ice now known
while I demurred wanting to
stay on our pale blue dot,
and it snowed that night
when we met one time ago.

Now years later into the
Anthropocene era I think
of you on this day when
the North and South poles
have melted down to ice cubes.
I will drop the first cube
into my last drink and
save the other to share
with you if you would

join me to commemorate
their final meltdown
in a martini glass,
while sitting alone
looking at the ice as
the shape of water and
now gone from the world.

I look up and you appear
from out of summer heat
wearing a teddy coat
and long Hermes scarf
and you sit close with me
to wait at Godot's Bar
for the return of winter
when we know all
will be well once again
when winter kept us warm and
covered earth in remembered snow,
that night when we met
some time ago.

TALES OF THE SHRUB

Part 1: Shrub's Chagrin

Tell me, O Shrub
as did Homer's muse
of the great exploits of Odysseus,
tell now three millennia later
at a time human civilization
faces chaos and extinction when
even Gaea no longer may be heard
about human beings exploiting this earth.

Yes, I do have tales to tell
starting with the prehistoric age
when your human species abided
by the laws of nature and
coexisted with other species evolving
in a world of ecological balance and peace

then devolving in this era of
your epochal rising over others
including my own pitiable species
eaten and trampled by marauding mammals
isolated in the barren soil of parched mesas
worn down by wind and heat
starved and stunted in arid land.

So I lie here supine before you
reduced from beauty to ugly
as a common weed of no regard
deemed useless as the lowest species
and primitive remnant from a bygone era.

Part 2: Shrub's Challenge

I have seen you arrive once hesitant
(with only weapons and tools of stone, then
making bronze and iron and great machines)
now treading dominant over the earth
your numbers multiplying by the billions
your sciences and technologies transforming
the elements given by nature while

devouring countless plant and animal species
tearing apart the fabric of ecological systems
depleting minerals and poisoning the land
draining aquifers and rivers for fields and lawns
heating global air by burning ancient life carbons.

So O Human
Do not speak in this late century
of your triumphant odyssey
over this earth facing chaos and extinction
during your vaunted Anthropocene Age
that promised unlimited frontiers and
and development of infinite resources.
Do not boast as the proud victor who

rendered extinct thousands of species,
yet who now comes meekly before me
as the forlorn refugee hungry and thirsty
in search of solace and guidance while

here on the high plains of Kansas
under a blistering sun of famine
while behind you the salted sea
creeps up the Mississippi River basin
in whose wake the Gulf coast cities lie
strewn and drowned by category six hurricanes.

Part 3: Shrub's Prophecy

Take heed of your existence as the last man
not just the past believer of gloried civilization
as Nietzsche once warned but as the
last survivor foretold in Revelations
about this earth of fragile life and finite size
ravaged by corporate chiefs and false prophets.

Tell what you now see
in this exhausted land now inhabited
by shrubs, shrubs everywhere, large and small
down from the mountains and arid plateaus
onto fields once fertile and cultivated for food
over what were glistening wheat fields of Kansas
and cornfields of Iowa under the once-blue sky
turned white and air shimmering with heat
and land cracked and dry without rain or aquifers

and native prairie grass withering away
to nourish only loathsome goats.

We shrubs have spread our species
from mountain tops heights to valley depths
over all continents of the earth
not surviving but thriving while
other species succumb to extinction

and we have thrived undaunted from
your civilization and industrial abuse
sowing the seeds for our descendants
conserving the gift of water and sanctity of soil
thriving eons before and after your desecrations
rising and falling as the earth exhales and inhales, and
persevering through the age that is uniquely yours
– the Sixth Extinction.

So I tell you
taking from Homer's tale of the human quest
not his heroes who obeyed Athena gladly
but you who have broken her covenant of peace
– all your doing.

THE RIVER

On a sunny day you walk along the Ohio's shore
and feel the water lapping at your feet
the same water now as two centuries ago
(the same despite what Heraclitus said)
flowing tirelessly by this abandoned clearing

and where you see the residue of works once made
by pioneers of industry and believers of manifest destiny
moving commerce down the river of the heartland
riding high on the mercantile tide of world trade –
coal, iron, gold, timber, grain, the stuff of empires.

Walk beyond the clearing through the trees and
you see high up the bluff and down to the river's edge
an elevator once powered by a steam engine
now rusted, slumped and twisted, pieces on the ground

larger than the ancient bones of a dinosaur
with its conveyor belt tailing unto the river
once in its time a modern human machine
made to feed on commerce then dreamt of.

In their day the steamboat queens ruled these rivers
their tall stacks emitting trails of smoke and soot
their whistles cheered at the docks of stripling ports
seeking civilization through the lanes of world commerce
a pig's ear for the silk of Japan or tea of England
– as Fulton's steamboats chugged in treacherous currents

starting in 1811 from Cincinnati to New Orleans
braving perilous times of explosive boilers and the
New Madrid quake causing the Mississippi to flow backward
ringing church bells in Boston where empire started (tea again)

 – as the steamboats bombarded forts on rebelling shores
following Grant's attack lines drawn on river maps
starting in 1861 from Cairo to New Orleans and Chattanooga
to restore the union and resume the westward empire

– as you now hear the horn of a modern tugboat and
low growling of its 27,000 horsepower diesel engine
pushing 12 barges loaded with shoes and hats from Italy,
machinery from Germany, computers and phones from China.

All seems tame as you see the sun set on the shore
of docks and boats and the water quietly passing
along channels crafted and engineered
by Army Corps dredges dikes dams and locks

yet the power of the Ohio never changes
as a force of nature beyond human endeavor
sweeping away the shorelines of enterprise
and breaking down the lanes of river trade.

Yes, if you stop and sit by this river long enough
you will see the remnants of history float by
– pieces of docks and towns, shoreline schemes and dreams–
dislodged and vanished from the soil of the heartland

washed away to bob without anchor on the surface
made homeless and now floating away as before
into the ocean where all things drown and
dissolve into water (the same as Thales said).

RIVER'S END

You seek to see the rapid flowing waters
of the Colorado River wild and free
so journey the path winding through high mountains

> toward an opening of promise yet
> through passage toward an augured vista
> upward under clouds hovering above.

You walk intrepid upon this path of
unknown consequence and look on high
as karma falls away and mind empties

> free from identities of who you are
> free to move anywhere in place or space
> unshaken by movement or change.

You walk across an open plateau
and come without warning to the edge
to look down into shadowy bowels the

> silver thread of the Colorado River
> flowing down off the Continental Divide
> by rock and over land to join the sea.

Once running fast and cutting deep the
river nourished life and furnished soil
but now a trickle tamed and tapered

waned of natural force and form by
desert lizards in bright hotels
seeking pleasure of gold and flesh

drained through mountain-high aqueducts
denigrated into sewage pools
by coastal sharks afar drunk with wine.

You lean too far to see the river's end
and fall as told in the koan story
to catch and hold a slim branch with your teeth.

Standing above you and the river
Kyogen calls to ask where is the true way
this sly old teacher who dares to forbear
your desperate attachment to the branch
and demands an unanswerable answer.

Hanging below you know as Kyogen knows
no answer can satisfy his question
and no branch can hold your dangling body
for the way is to denounce attachments
as the dharma and nature command.

So said, you descend into the void
down deep between the river's shores
your freedom from attachment complete
noted by Kyogen who bows and chants
gate paragate parasamgate.

You become one with the flow of the
Colorado River once wild and free
now trickling through a hostile terrain
waters stolen by white collar thieves to
nourish desert lizards and coastal sharks.

You are dried and drained away from life's flow
your way lost from high hopeful mountains
and lost to find waters flowing free
failing to find the sea of your true place
succumbing to the desert without trace.

CAT'S CRADLE

Lying with Kurt in the cat's cradle
we join in wondering why why why
about flying tigers and hunting birds and
how we and our karass can understand

we are incidental fallout from
the birthing cradle as the khōra
rocking back and forth unsuspended
moving all things to perish and emerge

    earth recycling life, decaying down and sprouting up
    water recycling, cleaning earth and replenishing air
    air recycling water, drying up and coming down
    fire recycling energy, burning matter and kindling life.

The cat once was here to rock the cradle
recycling earth water air fire
before we came and after we left
ceaseless tao giving no mind to us

    mother earth of sustaining yin
    father god of lightning yang
    big bang cause of primal provenance
    primal purpose of final providence.

We now are condemned to dance with death
as done in fires of Slaughterhouse Five
our innocence shrugged off as collateral damage
by unknown forces of universal flux.

So it goes, for us to try but cannot understand
for the Books of Bokonon are endless,
and now lying with Kurt in the cradle
I realize the cat was never here.

So it went.

KEYSTONE TALE

Once upon an eon there was the
beginning of the Phanerozoic

animals and plants evolved and emerged
in ecological harmony
thriving in a food chain of plenty
linking all species down to
bacteria absorbing sugar
and up to large cats digesting meat

each link known as the Keystone Species
for the stone at the center of an arch
holding in place the structure of life
and allowing no domination from
predators on high to destroy
links in the chain from below

until the Anthropocene Age
when the hominid mammal
forged tools as weapons of
stone, bronze and iron metal
and summoned by its god to be
fruitful and multiply in billions
to subdue the earth and
have dominion over all species

until none lived happily ever after
in a sad tale where very few lived at all.

EARTH ON FIRE

We stepped over the threshold

        too late to step back
        sliding down a slippery slope
        into the heat of fire below

        silent images flashing
        on reels of burnt celluloid
        of a world in fast motion.

We feel the heat of Greta's house on fire

        her teenage face of anguish
        foretelling hellish auguries
        in the heat of Swedish winter.

We see the Amazon River

        flowing to the ocean through
        a desert of burning sand
        carcasses strewn with stench.

We hear the Arabic guns

        thundering across the desert
        to the creaking of oil pumps
        and grinding of war machines.

We pass lines of people

walking on the waste land
silent and hollowed with
eyes fixed before their feet

on one side
thirsty refugees from oil and water wars
carrying AK Forty-Sevens

on the other
tired poor huddled masses yearning
to migrate into walled fortresses.

We plunge downward

with Brünnhilde riding
into the flames of Valhalla
Götterdämmerung!

with Dante into the Inferno
fallen from Virgil's guiding hand
where fire above joins fire below.

All the while Vulcan smiles from on high
seeing earth as a burning ring of fire

as green and blue
turn red and brown
blue Earth to red Mars
the sixth extinction set ablaze

this last by human ravaging
now of the Anthropocene Age

grasping earth in the palm of his hand

its course irreversible
no longer to be redeemed
by any of other gods

although Gaia tried
her followers languished
her spirit then vanquished

conceiving the advent of last throes

in the contradiction between
human desire unlimited
and earth's resources limited

auguries of innocence ravaged
eternity gone in an hour

as the blue dot turns red to gray.

All the while in smoldering ashes
Gaia weeps.

FATAL FLUTTER

So it was to be:
God created
Mindful humanity
Universal law
World perfected,
Amen.

So it came to be:
Butterfly fluttered
Wind rippled
Sky shuttered
World crippled,
So be it.

KERMIT'S DEMISE

Kermit died just yesterday
bathing in his favorite pan
failing to turn down the heat.

Reassured by caretakers
that the water would not boil
he failed to jump out in time.

Caretakers are being investigated
for fraud and dereliction of duty
in claiming the rising heat was a hoax.

Commemorative services
will be conducted to support
frogs still surviving worldwide.

Kermit is the subject of a movie script
written and titled by his family as
Out of the Pan into the Fire.

LOST UNIVERSE

HUBBLE'S EYE

Edwin Hubble saw far into night
      not stars but galaxies
      once seen only as stars

         two-hundred billion galaxies
         across ninety billion light years

         and to his astonished eye
         galaxies racing out to space
         at an ever-increasing pace.

He saw into the universe
      not in a steady state
      like a well-tuned engine

         but a runaway train
         dashing down a dark track

         going out to nowhere
         no end of space or time.

Einstein shook his head
      and said it cannot be
      so added lambda to the
      cosmological constant

         until the red light shift
         discovered green light speed
         out into the unknown.

Even Plato of old
                saw the universe destined to the
                eternal formlessness of khöra

                not something but nothing of form in
                space without edge and time without end.

Hubble lives on through his scope over earth
                seeing galaxies sail out to sea and
                disappearing beyond the horizon

                to an unknown there of when and where.

ETERNAL ENTROPY

Energy indestructible forms matter
by the first thermodynamic law of conservation:

> Vishnu creator of form:
> The Preserver making quanta magna
> particle to atom to element to molecule
> all bodies material and stellar.

Energy destructible deforms matter
by the second thermodynamic law of entropy:

> Shiva destroyer of form:
> fire from his third eye to burn
> the world as the ashes of his body
> presaged by his dance of death.

Brahma rules the universe of the Veda
completing the Hindu Trinity to
mediate thermodynamic laws and
uphold the supreme law of the advaita.

Yet entropy rules the universe of matter:
form yielding to force of energy
fusion surrendering to fission
light fading into the nothingness of darkness
dark matter scattering from dark energy
quantum forces dissipating in space-time
bosons trembling and constants wavering
the Higgs boson deflating
the cosmological constant inflating.

Entropy rules the world of human:
making heaven and earth not humane
treating ten thousands things as straw dogs
dressed in the ceremony of civilization
and then thrown unto the road to nowhere,
unable to congregate matter for mind
unable to aggregate the Boltzmann brain
as the possibility of reflective consciousness
as the impossibility of possibility.

Entropy laws and fuel are eternal:
Big Bang burns down to Deep Freeze
alpha of light to omega of darkness
stretched beyond the force of gravity
galaxies tossed and lost in oblivion
into the silent void of shapeless forms.

BLACK HOLE

You cannot see a black hole

    not one anywhere
    but it is still there.

All is deformed

    as the Lucretian swerve of matter
    entangling atoms and generating form

    becomes the Luciferian fall of matter
    disentangling atoms and degenerating form

    giant stars swallowed into fathomless depths of
    a black hole and vanished into a worm hole.

All is disappeared

    nothing escapes and returns
    even light is out of sight

    gone quarks and planets of matter
    leptons and stars of energy

    no place or distance of space
    event or duration of time.

You know all this is beyond physics
this absurd question of a black hole

for the answer lies in space-time gone
where nothing is ever seen or known.

Such thoughts swirl as you sit on a stool
head slumped down and drinking with drool and

hearing the sound of the midnight call
you drink the last glass of your muscatel and

staring at the bottom you quickly squirm
knowing the answer lies there in the worm

where nothing more can be seen or known
which is your moment of clarity.

MIDNIGHT MOON

Melancholia the movie of
the seventh last extinction
shows a rogue planet hurling
forth to end life on earth

coming as surely as gravity
steadily dropping
uncaring to crying and praying
never stopping.

With such thought of gloom
I now walk in mid-night
my feet stirring sleeping streets
dark houses with dim lights

a moth flitting into a streetlamp
receding sound of a lone train
red light blinking on a bald hill
all seeming to be right.

Yet danger looms this quiet night
with the moon full and shining silver
clipped by clouds large and colored black
casting shadows on the ground below
reappearing ever more large and near

as if unleashed by a broken thread
falling earthward in a dance of doom
maybe not tonight but gravity is the law
mass to motion without emotion

both moving through the night.
Oh moon speak to me
you fancied face of man
regulator of tides and turns
subject of song and verse,
heir of human homage
figure of heaven
son of Selena.

Say you are one of us
not a chaos-scripted planet
although four billion years ago
you were that when rogue
when worlds were in collision
in a universe of swirling dust
and form and life were void.

As we now meet again.
are you rogue again?
Please say you care
so as to spare us while
walking through the streets
looking up in the night
as children trusting Selena.

END-ALL

Lightning strikes, energy flashes.
The breaker breaks, the system crashes.
Vital signs stop, body shuts down.
All things end, nothing is found.

All stops:
sound to silence
sight to blindness
light to darkness
movement to stillness
universe of 14 billion years
earth of 4.5 billion years
hominid life of 3 million years.

All goes:
particles and elements
cells and life
earth and sky
stars and galaxies

light and energy
time and space
mind and matter
creator and creation.

The all starts and comes by each of us
done by a three-pound brain
as an omniscient mega-god
whether worthy or not.

The all ends and goes by each of us
done after a last heart beat
exhaled into oblivion by a last breath
whether deserved or not.

The world is our idea Schopenhauer said
and so will live and also die within our head.

The all depends upon us plus our circumstance
and the end will not be by accident or chance.

BETELGEUSE

on the right shoulder of Orion
with gigantic mass twenty times the sun
getting bigger and redder than all stars in the sky

this red super giant
with corona seams stretched to break
preparing the greatest supernova of the eon

ending ten million years
of growing pregnancy to be the mother
birthing stars and constellations for the future

occurring any time now
as the dazzling and ultimate fireworks show
lighting the galaxy to be seen across the unverse

yet sadly dying as
nature goes about recreating the new
and incurring collateral destruction of the old

which also would be us.

YEATS' THIRD COMING

O Yeats if you now knew of the
Big Bang and universe new
found and bound to be
turning and turning in a widening gyre
thrown into ever-widening space-time
as things fall apart and center cannot hold.

Yes, the black-dimmed energy is loosed, and everywhere
the ceremony of cosmic innocence is thrown
in all ten directions of cosmic intensity:
particles scattering like CERN-induced collisions
atoms disentangling and forms dismantling
energy bleeding from brown stars and black holes
galaxies bursting apart like nebulae.

So now you come to know
the last hour will occur
and third coming is at hand
so sail on to Byzantium
and what pleasures may be had
in a universe gone mad.

RELIGIOUS JOURNEY

YOU AND GOD

You can be as God

as much as you know

which is all out there

to know what is here

and God can be as you

as less as you know

which is all in here

to know what is there.

It is all for you

to give what is due

to reach what is far

to know what is more

and lines can break down

opened to be free

beyond boundless space

beyond seamless time.

God is up to you

and all more or less

as far as you reach

as much as you know

and you sure can be

(it's not a mystery)

always here and there

beyond space and time

to be free as God.

IDEA OF GOD

God is your idea as said

by Schopenhauer about the world.

You are God's idea as said

by Moses about the creation.

You are Leonard Cohen who

wants to travel with Him who has

touched your perfect body with his mind.

Your idea of God is manifest in many ways

    music of spheres

    painting of Sistine Chapel

    poetry of Rumi

    physics of bosons

    mathematics of constants

    light of energy and yang

mass of matter and yin

immanence of language

transcendence of spirit.

SO WHAT

Who knows the origins and destinies
of the universe, life on planets, or you and me?

Who or what hatched the Cosmic Egg
and what will be its fate – the Big Rip or Deep Freeze
or the Cyclical Crunch (keeps the universe going)?
And what about me?

Some one or thing has to know about me to come and go,
so let's call it God

but God is not talking maybe not even being
surely not existing like me as a being in time and place.

So what God knows is not disclosed but closed
and to know is egging me down here below.

So what?

GOD AND THE UNIVERSE

God came
fourteen billion years ago,
blew a lot of air
through a small hole
turned black into white
hot gas into energy
energy into particles and
particles into elements of matter.

God proclaimed
let there be light,
then entered a
wrong number for the
cosmological constant
turned energy into matter
matter into entropy and
entropy into the big freeze.

God explained
nothing went wrong,
took another chance
to make another
universe perfect
always steady state
in his image of
something called heaven.

God disdained
the universe gone bad,
left flawed in design
white turned into black
dark energy run rampant
center unable to hold
things breaking apart
into entropic oblivion.

God went
whereabouts unknown.

DEATH OF GOD

Per the death of God that came
Poor Nietzsche usually gets the blame
Proud Kant and Hegel deserved such fame
Postmoderns prat and prance about the same:

their airy vocabulary denies all exemplary
le tout autre expands infinity to naught
Derridian différance deconstructs substance
Baudrillarian simulacra banalizes the word.

Nietzsche knew with certainty
Who killed God was not he
But we.
Yes we.

We first created God as a wispy other etched on cave walls
    and talismans
Then gave God a human shape and personality as a creator,
    ruler, judge
To inspire prophets to idealize heaven and warriors to
    realize Armageddon
Then blamed and killed God as a theodic muddler of morality.

Where is the originary God undefiled by human history?
Perhaps lighting the fireworks of another Big Bang.
Perhaps as the absolute infinity of a unified field/world theory.
Perhaps beyond Chardin's Omega Point or an infinite algorithm.

Have we missed God in one place and failed to search
    another?
Perhaps God with Whitman stopped somewhere waiting
    for us.
Perhaps we sit with Godot and wait at the wrong place.
Perhaps we follow only Dante's Virgil and search the wrong
    realm.

Who knows the originary God
When not of our doing or undoing
But perhaps some essence of being
Existing still somewhere with us?

CROSSED IN EDEN

What went wrong in God's paradise of Eden
The covenant of eternal life and greatest deal humankind
    ever had
Then rescinded to bring on sin and death, a deal gone
    horribly bad?

Called upon to pass the test and never suffer evil
Adam put his faith in this God in whom he could rejoice
Adam the trusting fall guy, double-crossed, never had a choice.

Tempting Adam with serpent calls, apples, and Eve
God omniscient would feign surprise just as
God omnipotent would seal Adam's demise.

Adam was sacrificed in an angelic dispute
Made subject to Iblis lurking in outlays of hell
An Islamic back-story Genesis would not tell.

It never came to be for man to have eternity.
We must now live to die because God had bigger fish to fry.
It's only fair we no longer care that God also would die.

Such is the story within the story
Of the God man takes in then sends away
An all-too-human God who would betray.

After much is said and pages read
Any real story cannot be told.
No script valid lies beyond the fold.

GOD CHASE

God is the tail I chase in a circle
like a dog mistaking itself
for someone else.

As for God a circle does not matter
nor my mistaking someone else
coming back to myself.

As for me the circle will break
ending with no beginning
passing myself away.

I know only circles and squares
without an equation to
square the circle.

God knows the equation without fail
while I am the dog
chasing my tail.

A BELIEVER

I believe in
life
peace
knowledge
power
freedom.

I believe God is
immortality
eternality
omniscience
omnipotence
omnipresence.

I believe in being God
and nothing less.

God is what I believe
and nothing more.

I'm a believer.

THE BELIEVER

Most people think the Trinity odd:
Does Jesus still live as Spirit and God?
Jesus was a Jew but Jews are not sure;
on Jesus as Spirit and God they demur.

According to John, Christ lived on
canonized as God's only son
who set oceans and continents afire
salvation wrought by soldiers of empire.

Jesus became Christ and Christ Christendom:
good news for believers of Christ to come
but not so when heard by followers like me
who love only Jesus of Galilee.

THE DOUBTER

Oh death where is thy sting?
Though I walk through the
valley of the shadow of death
I fear no evil.

            -Bible, Psalms 23

So I'm walking . . .

down here . . .

still farther . . .

more shadows . . .

getting dark . . .

path gone . . .

so what . . .

spooky folktale . . .

stupid talk . . .

stupid walk . . .

seen enough . . .

coming back up . . .

just step over this

a
  b
    y
      s
       s
        . . . .

DUKE AND GOD

John Wayne
on his deathbed
summons a priest,
prays and confesses
to receive Catholic baptism,
anointing and Viaticum
for the first time of his life.

He takes this one chance
to obtain absolution
to repent his sins and
absolve his pagan past
for the last time in his life.

Later that day he mounts his horse
and rides off into the sunset
up to his final roundup
in technicolor.

Amen, Pilgrim.

SPARE THE PRAYER

The prayer addressing God all bountiful
still could spare God from praying for salvation.

Surely God would favor meditators
asking only to be tuned into the moment
wanting nothing and happy with emptiness
seeking reincarnation with no celestial overhead.

Spare the prayer.
God will be thankful.

SPIRITUAL JOURNEY

OPENINGS

There is a crack in everything, which is
how the spirit gets out from the
shell of self and thought of ego

from between the edges
of the vise closing down the
distance of space and duration of time

from the pleasure and pain of body
out into the limitless space of mind
where ideas are openings.

Even black holes leak energy
a photon at a time – drip, dripping
out into empty space

their information never lost
as photons unite with protons
recombined to illuminate the darkness
– a star is born.

Martin Luther King rises from
the caste of mind made black by white
to speak of justice for all
who ride together on the rainbow
of colors seen throughout the universe
– free at last.

God sends the avatar
coming through the haze of blue turned gray
to save the earth once green burned brown
as a last chance roll of the dice
in a casino locked down by billionaires.

Opening of openings
all is opening
to those locked away outside who hear
calls whispered through the air
from a spirit without body or name

who see refuges shining in the mist
wherein boundaries fade away
blessed by light coming straight through space-time
unhindered by gravity of black holes

and who live without death or birth
existing in all four dimensions and ten directions
where possibilities are infinite.

SUPERSOUL

It's here and now and there and then
beyond a given place and time
abiding in each breath of air
hiding within plain sight sublime.

It's super, trans, pan, omni, preter, prima, über
the whole of every part, substance of every soul

        supersensory, beyond
        seeing, hearing, feeling, smelling or tasting

        superlinguistic, beyond
        talking, writing, thinking or imaging

        supernatural, beyond
        matter, energy, space or time, and life

        superspiritual, beyond
        prayers, scriptures, avatars, and gods.

It's Spinozian substance extended
to and through all things, so to be

        infinite and immutable
        and attributes eternal

        independent from any other thing
        and never to be known completely.

Not caused, created, aligned, relative
it is the primal origin and sole source

        singularity of plurality
        first light of the cosmic egg

        spawning forth the universe
        pushing forward space and time

        provenance of beginning
        and providence of ending

        the khöra of Plato
        and dao of Lao Tzu.

Not the consequent of mind and thought
it is the antecedent of mind and thought

        light waves of all colors
        and energy range of all rays

        air waves carrying to ears
        the motion of perfect sounds

        mirror reflecting to eyes
        true image of perfect forms

        formless form of the absolute
        emptiness of "no" and being of "is"

shapeless shape of shapes and
design hidden in chaos.

Not this, that, or the other thing
it is what it is and all of what is.

. . . .

Supersoul first shone forth as dawn of the Axial Age
primal light seen twenty-five hundred years ago
eternal monolith of nondual consciousness
infinite truth of perennial philosophy

soul of Plato in Greece
nirvanic soul of Buddha in India
energy soul of Dao in China
soul of Zoroaster in Persia.

The East upheld wholistic souls
not divided dual or triune
sparkling across Indra's jeweled net
of interdependent harmony.

From the old gods of the Israelites
through the holy spirit of Jesus
the West gave substance to sacred souls
canonized by church saints and prophets.

The Western soul became secularized
pursuant to the theory of everything

all things dreamt of in the sciences and
the four forces detected in physics.

Americans heard Emerson's over-soul
emanating out of New England churches
and Whitman's adventurous soul venturing
across the spacious plains of a new world.

Supersoul shines as the ceaseless dawn of all ages
energy from matter, consciousness from energy
plain as day yet dazzling throughout the universe
seen and known to all sentient souls as Supersoul.

. . . .

Mystics skeptical of sacred souls
still seek out Supersoul in plain sight
contemplating a grain of sand in hand
and eternity in a human hour.

Mystics heed Meister Eckhart to stop
about themselves and complaints for favors
to listen and let in the energy
already given twenty-four seven.

Unfathomable to the human mind
Supersoul cannot be invented
only discovered and partly so
primal before and final after.

Supersoul transcends boundaries known as
incompleteness of Godel's number logic
infinity of Russell's set theory and
uncertainty of Heisenberg's principle.

. . . .

You are more than energy
scattered across formless fields
timeless flickering of string theory

more than Heisenberg probability
more like Einstein dice of certainty
always rolling up seven.

You are the mass of matter
the body of created form
by the Higgs particle of God

the perfect universal form
the Vitruvian man of De Vinci
where circles and squares are one

the Mandelbrot fractal of
all forms of mass to matter
of eternal divine design.

CHAIN OF BEING

The universe is always the same
after you go and before you came.

The first law of thermodynamics
sees the conservation of matter and

leptons streaking safely in space as
indestructible information even

from black holes. The second law of
thermodynamics sees matter deform

as energy and energy reform
as air, water and earth of matter.

The theory of abiogenesis
sees the molecules of oxygen,

hydrogen, nitrogen and phosphorus
evolve as bacteria, then to

multiple-celled Eukaryotes, to central
nervous systems with sensory organs,

to limbic and mammalian brains, and to
symbol-making minds, all by the laws of

infinite emergence and complexity
transcending the evolution of life itself

from the actuality of phylogenesis
to the potentiality of ontogenesis.

The chain bends into a circle back to
ashes of matter and energy as

alternating complexity of Lucretian
atoms entangled and disentangled

and back to the life and death of
organisms and universes

all reenactments of Nietzsche's
doctrine of eternal return.

The chain sparkles like Indra's net
with each jewel a portal to stars

glistening to show the way
perhaps to the opening of the Tao

perhaps to the Platonic khōra
or Tillichian God beyond gods

all pointing beyond human being
to primal being never seen and known

beyond existence of having and doing
beyond the edge of space and end of time.

Although no link in the unbreakable chain
no start or end in the unfathomable chain,

you want to ride the train down the chain to
enter the mysteries of primal being

from whence all things come and all things go
never to be yours to see and know.

WHITMAN'S SONG

The American dream came after the morning
of the Great Awakening and with the day
glistening of the vistas of sprawling seaports
and railroads laid across green plains and
through western heights of purple mountains
under skies open to an endless frontier

all celebrated through the poems of
Walt Whitman as an outpouring of self
not the transcendental self of Emerson
nor the pedestrian self of Wordsworth

but a self of the earth, leaves and grass
of good health to filter and fibre the blood
of common working men and nurturing women
of the American free soul and democratic spirit

a self of consciousness beholding life
beyond quotidian words or ideas
something still beyond real and ideal
from a thousand miles and nowhere found

moving in the wind from western frontiers
calling to come forth from faraway plains
fertile and inviting, feral and waiting:
I stop somewhere waiting for you.

He still sings his beckoning song
stopping somewhere on the long island
then known as Paumanok by native people

where grass still grew and leaves adorned
where the air was clear and water pure
where the virgin wonders of nature still stirred.

His song now fades on this Long Island
and unreal city of concrete waste land

its buildings scraping sky and blocking sun
lighting the night and dimming once bright stars
its sidewalks bustling with bodies fast-forward
hustling and busting out one door into another

its boulevards streaming with steel vehicles
emitting noxious fumes of roaring engines
its ports filled with ships spewing forth boxcars
of goods from global expropriation

its economy working people
not harvesting the grass of nurture

its culture fashioning people not
celebrating the leaves of nature.

But listen and you still may hear those
murmurings of Whitman in your ear
meant for all the people of your day
whose American dream has gone astray.

WALK WITH BUDDHA

Walk with the Buddha into Nirvana
where world suffering is blown out
casting away the winds of karma and
quelling the desire of life and fear of death.

Walk into the dwelling of the three refuges:
Buddha's fourth jhana of pure equanimity
Dharma's release from life and death of samsara
Sangha's meditative silence and oneness.

Walk the path of no boundaries
covered by leaves of change on formless grass
beneath trees of seeds blown into space
marked by pure light empty of shadows.

Walk upon the freely moving wind
rising feet never touching defiled ground
levitating into endless space and time
joining ten thousand things in ten directions.

Walk through the emptiness of form
with no adjacent space of here and there
or sequential time of now and then
and with body and mind left behind.

Don't walk, no steps really needed
sit and abide in destinations
already here in your motionless mind
through which walking comes and goes.

WALK WITH LAO TZU

Walk with Lao Tzu not there
like the Tao not here
but everywhere.

You know without knowing
Tao must be unknown
to be everlasting.

You name without naming
Tao to be named by
metaphors not lasting.

When severed from Tao
you walk with the mother
of ten thousand things.

When united with Tao
you walk into the origin
of heaven and earth.

Tao is like wood
when uncarved left for good
when carved used for evil.

Tao is the cosmic egg
from which all things emerge
to which all things return.

Tao is the great sponge
dripping out the water of life
absorbing the decay of death.

Tao is the pure calm
before the storm of action
when nature is inhumane.

Tao is what it is
not for you to have
because it has you.

Walk with old Lao Tzu
knowing and trusting
Tao is life's primal goo.

WALK WITH RUMI

Walk with Rumi upon the desert road
where caravans travel on endless roads
of silken belts and splendid caliphates
when their journey pursues the visions of
Arabian nights

          and Scheherazade seeks
love to be at the end of the road
where mystics told tales of love and wrath.

For believers, the road is formless
no longer attached to the ground as
rock dissolves to sand and sand to air
and air to spirit

          and no words heard
of rules by mullahs and sharia law
no counts of stars in the universe
or grains of sand upon desert dunes.

For believers, the road is selfless
no longer different from the other
nor separate as the part from the whole
or cause making the effect

          for the one is
ten thousand things and they are you
though Shams said you don't understand.
So be a believer in the mystic path
and walk with Rumi through space of no distance

traversing the world in all ten directions
no sign heeded, no compass needed
all marked paths of the past left behind
the pathless path

                       as the wind blows
over pathways, crossroads, trodden routes
across blue oceans and brown continents
between earth poles of white

                       as the wind
blows through space-time of the universe
suspending the force of gravity and
moving galaxies beyond dimensions
in a game of bocce

                       as you ride the wind
detached and free even of Rumi (but
not to worry for he will understand)
and dissolve into the water of life,
earth of birth, energy of fire
and air of freedom

                       for all the elements
are of you and you are of them as you
abandon form and become pure spirit
in the infinite here and eternal now.

WALK WITH JESUS

You want to walk with Jesus
down the Mount of Olives road
laden with clothing by those

who love you as their father
who loves them in return

but be careful who you walk with.

Your destination is Jerusalem
yet you tremble at its danger

darkened by the imperial power of Rome
deprecated by the Pharisees jealousy
desecrated by greed within the Temple.

Your destiny is Calvary
yet the hill of crucifixion

where you want to be remembered
there with him to forgive them
who know not what they do.

You want to walk in his footsteps
into the history of his name as

the messiah of love and peace
although the road is dangerous

the chosen son of the holy Father
although the body is sown with sin

the anointed saint whose soul is perfect
although in the end feeling forsaken.

No, you cannot walk in his footsteps
to find the way

but you can fall upon your knees
to seek and pray.

KILL HIM

If you see the Buddha, kill him, Lin Chi shouted
lineages ago during Buddhism's Golden Age.

Harsh but true about any heralded arhat
since the only living Buddha is within
you are killing only your delusion.

Even Christians warn about craven images.
So, kill the Christ, it is only just and fair.

As for Jesus, he walks with you and the Buddha
down the path to the same altar upholding
the mysteries of Heaven and Nirvana.

LET HIM GO

From the trees of Jetta Grove
the Buddha whispers in my ear:
Let Mara go, as things come and go
the good and bad that would be had.

Oh one to revere
I have not him.
He has me, and
will not let go.

Oh do not fear
he has your self.
If you let go
he has nothing.

The whisper fades back into the trees
before a breeze that clears all karma
free from attachment to good and bad
as all things go when no longer had.

WATER BIRD

The anthropic principle must
include the law of entropy

for a universe scattered wide
of gravity and energy

for sentient beings depending
on the law of conservation.

All of this matters
when the way is lost

when all form shatters
and dimensions tossed, yet

a bird from water flies
away leaving no trace

and always will know where
to go to find its place.

Jim (James Michael) Hanson is a retired Senior Researcher at Southern Illinois University-Carbondale, where he worked and taught in economic and community development. He resides in the St. Louis area. He has a doctorate degree in sociology and is an ordinated Zen Buddhist. In past years he has published two books through Greenwood Publishing Group and more than twenty articles in the social sciences. He is a member of the St. Louis Poetry Center and Illinois State Poetry Society-Southern Section, participating in workshops and readings. A chapbook was published by Flutter Press in 2019 and titled *Anthropic Musings: Poems on Human Survival in the Coming Extinction.* Recent single poems have appeared in *The Avenue, Black Cat, Coastal Shelf, Dissident Voice, Harbinger Asylum, I am not a silent poet, International Journal of Fear Studies, Nebo, Nightingale and Sparrow, New Verse News, Otolith, Parsec Ink, Poetry24, River Poets Journal, Sacred Journey, Writers Resist.*

This project was made possible, in part, by generous support from the Osage Arts Community.

Osage Arts Community provides temporary time, space and support for the creation of new artistic works in a retreat format, serving creative people of all kinds — visual artists, composers, poets, fiction and nonfiction writers. Located on a 152-acre farm in an isolated rural mountainside setting in Central Missouri and bordered by ¾ of a mile of the Gasconade River, OAC provides residencies to those working alone, as well as welcoming collaborative teams, offering living space and workspace in a country environment to emerging and mid-career artists. For more information, visit us at www.osageac.org

Osage Arts Community